Spirit Birds

Mary Oishi

Spirit Birds They Told Me

WITHDRAWN

Some of these poems have previously appeared, sometimes in slightly different versions, in anthologies of New Mexico poets: *Harwood Anthology*, *Looking Back to Place*, and *Earthships*.

Most have appeared in small press poetry magazines, nuclear resistance calendars, newspapers, or on-line publications, among them dukecityfix.com and decirdelagua.com.

Some were on *Kiss the World Awake*, a 2004 audio CD produced by Poetry Television, and some were performed on KUNM-FM public radio in New Mexico.

All have been performed live at one time or another, at venues including the 60th Anniversary of Hiroshima Commemoration; "Mightier Than the Sword: Writers Address the Nuclear Age"; "Stir: A Festival of Words" (at the University of New Mexico), the Duende Poetry Series, and the Church of Beethoven.

First edition, January 2011
Paperback 978-0-9826968-3-5

Book and cover design by Alyssa Christy
Crane photograph: Jess Alford
Author photograph: Kyle Zimmerman Photography

Spirit Birds They Told Me is the eighth volume in the West End Press New Series, featuring full-length titles by emerging and more recognized authors.

For book information, see our web site at www.westendpress.org.

1/ichi. twentieth century silk

2/ni. white sheets, heavy blankets

3/san. out of shadows, up from graves

4/shi. thirst quenched

Dedication

To my 9th grade English teacher, Nancy Bieber, who saved my life.

To Margaret Randall, who tenaciously prodded me to complete this book.

To all of the other extraordinary women writers who bring their wisdom and inspiration to Sunday Salon in my home each month.

To Chizu "One Thousand Cranes" Oishi.

To Aja "One Who Cannot Be Conquered" Oishi, the newest link in the centuries-unbroken chain of strong Oishi women.

Prologue

My partner ran in waving a thick envelope. "You just got something from your mother!" That was the day in 1987 when I won the lottery, or so it felt. Inside the envelope was a cassette tape from my mother, who had contacted me fewer than five times in my entire life.

The tape began: "So many times I try write you but my English no good." She proceeded to explain everything she was feeling for the past thirty years. She laughed, she cried, she sang a Japanese song. As I said, I felt like I won the lottery. I had just changed my name to her family name, Oishi. Apparently that's what it took for her to understand what years of Mother's Day calls, birthday cards, and holiday gifts couldn't seem to convey.

The cassette tapes flew quickly back and forth across the continent. I told her what life was for me growing up with my father's relatives. She recalled her childhood in Japan before the war, talked about her marriages, about raising my two brothers, about her year in rural Pennsylvania where I was born, where the cash registers would stop and everyone would turn and stare at her until she left the store. Having grown up there, I knew she was telling the truth—and probably not telling the half.

I visited her three times from 1987 until she died two years later. It was during those visits I learned what it really means to be the child of an American soldier and a Japanese civilian from World War II: each wounded in a way that skews judgment and wrenches violence from the gentlest of souls. I learned why I endured a childhood that from this vantage seems completely unendurable. I saw with my own eyes where I got the strength.

After my mother died and before I moved here, I visited my Aunt Haruna in Albuquerque. She was also a war bride. She told me that most Japanese names ended in "ko." She said her mother, my grandmother, didn't want any of her children's names to end in "ko." She selected all of her children's names based on their meaning. My mother's name was One Thousand Cranes.

New Mexico. The natives of this place call it Aztlan, Land of the Cranes. Aztlan has taken me under its wing and nurtured me as a poet since I arrived here. It honors me as I stand on its stages and behind the microphones of its public radio station. Although twice colonized, this place retains a distinctly Latin American regard for its poets, a genuine respect akin to that of my Japanese ancestors.

New Mexico also has a profound connection to the Pacific Theater of the war that brought my parents together. Many of its elderly fought in the Philippines, just as my father did. And it was here that Oppenheimer and the other scientists secretly invented the nuclear bomb. My mother's people were the only ones to ever experience its monstrously genocidal power.

While living here I met Shigeko Sasamori, one of its casualties: hosted her in my home, interviewed her, and wrote about her. Through my association with Shigeko, I met the L.A. Bureau Chief from Japan's most widely-read newspaper, Yomiuri Shimbun. Because of the article she wrote telling the story of my mother, the war bride, and what happened to her and to her only daughter in America, I was able to return to Japan and give a speech to an auditorium of 400 students, faculty, and administrators, about the lingering effects of World War II and the absolute necessity for peace.

It is ironic that I could return in such an honored way when my mother felt she could never go back for the shame of marrying the enemy. It was an amazing experience to build that bridge seventeen years after my mother's death.

I've been told that poets *are* bridges. That rings so true for me. A bridge spans every imaginable divide from a small stream to a wide chasm. It does not either ignore or fall prey to the obstacle; rather, in the spanning it transforms from danger to possibility, from far-removed to a chance to know and understand. There were many huge divides in my life besides the estrangement from my birth family and my Japanese heritage. It was necessary to build a bridge from white supremacist brainwashing to the genuine belief in the equal worth of all human beings; from abuse, neglect and disrespect to a healthy sense of self; from a paralyzing shame that literally "dare not speak its name" to being completely at ease in the knowledge that my same-gender attraction is as innate and value-neutral as my left-handedness and green eyes.

These bridges, decades in the making, take only minutes to cross. I am honored that you will cross them with me, daughter of One Thousand Cranes.

Mary Oishi

twentieth
century
silk

Tokyo unTold

This poem is dedicated to the more than 100,000 civilians who lost their lives on March 10, 1945, in the firebombing of Tokyo, during which nearly half a million bombs filled with 1665 tons of napalm were dropped continuously on sleeping Tokyo by over 1000 American military aircraft, leaving over 1 million survivors homeless, leaving almost nothing standing in over 16 square miles, and leaving the rivers and canals boiling and teeming with the dead. My mother, Chizu Oishi, survived this horror. This poem is also a loving tribute to her.

you never said they used napalm
you never told me that, mom

the day i found out {in an email}
was the same day i came down with
the worst flu i had in 30 years
my co-workers said i looked ashen
i know i didn't quite make it to the commode
i was retching, retching! god was i sick

they used napalm!
you never told me that, mom

aunt haruna told me:
me and your mother we were
watching our neighbor boy
he went crazy with all the bombing
he kept going out and waving at the airplanes
me and your mother we were watching
laughing at him he was so crazy
then somebody leaned out of one of the airplanes
and took his head right off
with a machine gun tat-tat-tat-tat just like that
then she laughed that laugh that used to
enrage the soldiers in vietnam,
you know that laugh, mom
like it's all too horrible like
you either run out and wave at airplanes
or you're two sisters howling from across the street

you never said they used napalm
there's a lot you never told me, mom

what you did say stays with me
fresher than september eleventh
though i thought of it again that morning
when i saw the people running terrified
their faces full of ash
what would they do if it was all of manhattan
i thought, if the planes kept coming
then they'd know what my mother knew

the morning's shocking news
sinks down in the guts by afternoon
and for me every afternoon is still
the afternoon of that day you told the story

i'll never forget it if i live to be a hundred

we just had quite the day in japantown
you telling the shopkeepers: domo arigato
i used to buy lots of tapes with just one music
you said, but then he tell me
why you not get this one—it have twenty music
more cheaper, most cheapest one
so now i buy this one tape, get twenty music

we go have sushi lunch downstairs by the moat
i watch you stack your tiles/amazed that
such a tiny woman can eat so much
it was delicious—it was a good day mom, remember?

on the bay bridge i asked that fateful question,
the one my brothers never asked
what was it like, mom? the war, what was it like?

oh, the planes just keep coming,
all night long, never stop
i was running through the streets,
everywhere buildings on fire, whole city burning
i was jumping over dead bodies as i run—
girls my age, old people, little children
i not know why i was running
anywhere i run to just as dangerous as
where i run from, i just run in sheer terror
nobody could clean anything up
and the stench! aw! it was the worst smell
i ever smell, worst smell you could imagine

4

i just keep running and telling myself
I'VE GOT TO LIVE!

i told your sons the night before you died
but i didn't say anything about napalm
i didn't know they used napalm
you never told me that, mom

i guess you couldn't remember
or maybe you never knew
it took so long to tell me anything at all

waiting for the flight to tokyo

BART is crawling along the hem of the hills
a raven takes off straight and unflinching
across the rooftop from the airport cafe window
everything is pointed east far east moving
i am reading ruth ozeki's *my year of meats*
trying to understand like the protagonist
my mixed heritages my disparate
cultural inheritance *me* ingredients
i am practicing my japanese phrases
practicing the speech i will deliver in english
a language of none of my ancestors
but the first one i learned
the only one i know without thinking
the sun has yet to set on that empire i think
on and on goes the conquest
the colonizing and i am the product
of a johnny-come-lately wouldbe colonizer
getting smacked down by the empire's
ruthless child lawless child
my father naive young farmer's son
believing in the story told to the poor
to the ones who lay down their lives
who take lives viciously to keep it marching
{god save the queen}
my mother charming daughter
charming damaged daughter of the upstart empire
witness to war crimes too horrible
to speak for decades
both with kindness still
holding outpost in their hearts
passed on to their children
along with the anger the violence
the clenched fists
and here i am trying to end world war II at last
trying to halt the marching
heal the wounds
traverse the distance between
san francisco and tokyo
plant seeds in the fading footprints of
mac arthur's men of truman's treachery
planting gentle seeds in the soft rend
of my own heart

my first morning in japan i am wakened

my first morning in japan i am wakened
by the call of a bird unlike any i ever heard
ahl arrrr arrrr it calls midflight
like it is heralding the dawn through a bamboo tube
another bird answers in less dreamlike shrill chirps
happy acknowledgements
my daughter stirs slightly
smiling in her sleep
happy on this futon in this
pleasant stark room
shoes arranged neatly outside the door
bless her for coming here in the first place
for giving me this extra incentive
so i would finally go back to my rice paddies
as the schoolkids once demanded

i saw my first rice paddies
in their neat little flooded rows
yesterday from the train window
last night i saw my first rows of lanterns
over the night streets
just like the ones in that mysterious
old photograph my mother left behind
the one with a dot penciled
over one head in the crowd
but nobody knows who it is
and she's not here to tell anymore

i thought i would be overcome with emotion
thought my heart would pound
at the first sight of its shoreline
thought i would want to kiss its ground
as soon as i landed
but the trip was grueling
the immigration line long long long
too much hassle to allow the sentimental
romantic homecoming i imagined

yet as i walked the back streets of
tokyo's working class neighborhoods last night
encountered a festival with its food and
games of chance   tubs of aquarium fish
smiling children   bonzai trees

stunning white flowers
as i walked among faces so varied
in features and skintone yet all japanese
i felt at ease in a strange way
like i was among relatives
people who smiled at me broadly

i thought of mom running
down such corridors of fire
when everything safely familiar turned
furnace by the american planes overhead
i wondered if the old ones in their kimonos
tried not to remember
if it was so much trying
that put a sober kind of sadness
in their aging eyes

it was at time for flying a time for birds

it was a time for flying a time for birds
a raven whisked me off from san francisco
a raven greeted me in tokyo
a flock were waiting in the trees of nara
each one a mystic shade of black

back at the base of the sacred mountain
a single swallow binked her beak
into the window near my bed
bink bink
bink bink
repeatedly
calling me into the dawn dreams
of japan at five a.m.
softer than a mother's heartbeat
consistent like taiko
bink bink
bink bink
wake up to ancestral memory
wake up to the history you were never told
welcome to it
another cultural reality
so long survived
so civilized
yet they too know so much pain
many still go out the old way   with honor
out of courage or just overwhelmed
with the weight of life

but those birds
those birds
those spirit birds they told me things
i never would have known

how hearts can follow
across oceans, mountains
hurts of the past
how we can fly and soar
so many different ways
how all our varied songs come from
the same place of longing
how there's so much beauty
even in the saddest call

fifty-three stations of tokaido

mother, slowly atoning for doing
what you had to do
given what you saw when you were in your homeland
given what you had to give up to marry the enemy
given you could never go home again
given you were repeatedly betrayed
and, after nearly forty years in america
still died a stranger

yet you stretch yourself from beyond to make amends
to bring me back to your motherbreasts
by bringing me back to the womb of what made you
by sending me an emissary from your war-gouged generation
whose heart even a nuclear weapon could not destroy
she assured me you loved me
she said you loved me so much in fact
that's why i was so drawn to you
that your love yearned me into seeking it
all the way across the continent
that's what i feel so strongly
she told me with the conviction of a saint

i believed her then
i believe her now
because it's still reaching me
across the divide between
life and mystery
across the generations
calling my daughter to japan
so i would follow
calling their reporter to my door
calling me to return as more than tourist
but speechmaker, poet, hungry-hearted lost child
finding my way to the seed of me
ancient cherry-blossomed spawning place
for half of me (always buried
just beyond where i could see)
only glimpses in books
in a few artifacts left behind
but always two-dimensional and fairy tale

then to ride a bike down the raised paths
between its rice paddies!

for fuji to preside over the actual horizon
instead of lying flat and mute
between the mat, behind the glass
to be greeted in her language
touch her fabrics, smell her rivers after a rain
ride her fast train, her shinkanzen
hurling down the ancient path
on my way to kyoto
with hiroshige's 53 stations of tokaido
muffled over loudspeakers
as stops along the route

now not one memento of your japan
would be flat for me
not even on the thinnest paper
it is forever raised far more than bas-relief
those memories, mythical pageants
a pilgrimage to heal

now that i am back home
on the continent where you birthed me
(then lost me)
where even after reconciliation and death
you are not done yearning me
to your motherbreasts
you move one who loves me
to give me her inheritance
to feel it, call it, make it mine
hiroshige's 53 stations of tokaido
in an old silk crane-bound book
of the one thousand cranes you were
you sent me a few engraved on its cover
when i opened its pages i wept

this is my inheritance

a print of fuji in autumn
another of fuji in spring, flooded ricefields below
i hung them up right away
they bring back scenes for me, yes
but more, they bring me peace
japan has come to visit me
the old one you remember
you have come with it, mother
smelling of early twentieth century silk

for Hachiko

i'm too curious
i could not stand for years by
the station waiting

white sheets,
heavy blankets

flat earth/white people

mom used a lot of bleach
when she washed her sheets
they came out really really white

salt is white

before the dogs get to it
snow is white

clouds are sometimes gray
but the big puffy ones
are always white
i used to lie on the ground so still
i thought i could feel the earth
slowly turning under them

mom's parents used to
sew those sheets into robes
and pointed hats
because they thought they themselves
were white
thought god was white
even told me i was half white

they learned this
from their ancestors
who never ventured this way
until the earth
had finally become round
for several centuries

guess they never got real still
under the clouds or
in front of the mirror

father's day

i heard a man whistle a strong tune in a parking lot
my dad whistled so much Whistle was his nickname

funny how you hate your dad so intensely
you plot ways to kill him just prior to falling into adolescent sleep

yet—you love your dad so much that a decade after his death
your impulse is to run to a whistling stranger

raised by wolves

i am a child peering out from under guilty tables
in dark rooms with the blinds drawn
but the guilt is not mine
my mother pulled me in there
crouching down and shushing me
hiding from the bill collectors
who pounded the old wooden screendoor angrily
we know you're in there,
you tell your husband if he doesn't pay by friday
we're calling the sheriff
i was ready to come out from under that table
emerge from that dark room
stand on this side of the screendoor
and face them
the guilt is not mine
but she shushed me and held me there and
shook her head firmly no!
she knew she was draining his money
for her *medicine* as she called it
the morphine that put her
in a stupor and eased her pain
the doctors kept her hooked on it
years after her surgery
the guilt is not mine nor hers to bear
the men drugged and raped her
sixteen with a hysterectomy
bastard child of a poor miner
the men raped me without medication
nine and ten and eleven and thirteen
halfbreed heathen child
and did they ever crow and preen in church!
no the guilt is not mine
in those blacked out bedrooms
with their firmly shushed secrets
where saints turn to werewolves
pretty little heathen girls to prey
the guilt is not mine
the guilt is definitely not mine
the guilt was never ever mine

redemption song

its voice was much like mine
alto, lower than the violins
i sat in rapt attention as
the man on stage played on
music so unlike the raucous mountain gospel
clapped in my sunday ears
no, these rich winds lifted me up from RD 2
from where a few familiar cars drove by
this music whooshed god off his throne
sat me there awhile without
the faintest air of disrespect

i knew that i *must* learn to play

the ones who raised me
never had to scold for me to practice
i gladly tried to glide that bow with
grace enough to lift me up again
out of eighth-grade-is-the-highest-you-can-go
out of this world where satan lurked
in all things fun and beautiful

one thousand days of private paradise until
a proud if stilted night when
"mom and dad"
awkward as catfish in their sunday finest
sat rigid in their friday seats
clapped only when the others did
for me up there so small
playing pizzicato next to college kids
in fiddler on the roof
long way from when i came home second grade
excited, begging
they agreed to let me play
an instrument whose name
they never heard before
what is it again, viola?

viola was my only place to go
where pearl harbor never happened
where white was not the standard
japanese was not a shame
where everyone could spend the night

unharmed despite their size
shape of their eyes or
color of their skin

words can be knives as sharp and swift
as swords from grownups mouths
the principal that fifth grade day
your parents must not care about you
very much   they have not paid
you must surrender your viola
instructor like a guillotine chimes in
his overkill   it's such a shame
good as you are

they brought home a big brown handled case
holding their hoped-for redemption
a plain old wurlitzer accordian
of yellowed celluloid not pearly black or red
like those italian ones i'd often seen
i put the straps around my sighing arms
taught myself to play out from the c chord button
with no rhinestone, just an unassuming
dent to mark its place

to this day accordians sound like disgrace to me

yet when i run across one in a thrift store
i can't resist the urge to play
to resurrect those long gone eyes so full of sorry
to play one happy little song that makes them smile
because they did the best they knew
because four strings are not
the only way to get to god

old spice

he took the tickles to a level of terror
almost smothered me in a pile of blankets
under 230 pounds of muscle and bone

gave me measled cheeks with many whisker rubs
manipulated me with foreplay games
an adult woman could have appreciated

imaginative

homestretch of the game was always the same
a massive chest coming down
at my little face

he took the tickles to a level of terror
vicious play, vicious icky play
i had no other playmates, no protector

anything is survivable if that's how life simply is
the smallest chest heaves for air
amid crushing secrets and old spice

no more nails

in the woods with his logging crew
a log swung out of the mechanical claws
straight across his chest
smashed his heart and lungs
crushed the life out of 6 foot 6
in his thirties
father of three
it was just before easter

i went to the funeral
because i knew he was the darling
of his three older sisters
because they told me his mother wailed
my son, my son, my son!
i knew her health was already broken
against the walls she was thrown into
by a raging son-in-law and
she was closer to me than my blood grandmother

i went for her, for them

but i never would have gone
had i known the near lynching that awaited me
his widow, tugging on me
oh mary, we just had a revival meeting and
joseph said he would do whatever it takes
to get little mary back to god
even if it meant his life
you must repent
not only did jesus die for you
but joseph died for you too
the crowd gathered around me
five or six deep on every side
while she made this tearful plea

patti smith sang *jesus died for somebody's sins*
but not mine

joseph died for his own sins
of this I'm sure
sins committed on an innocent child
sins he was afraid *i* would confess

hardly an easter passes when i don't think
of the giant cross mainbeam
that came off that truck to take him down
hardly an easter passes when i don't remember
my own near crucifixion at the hands of
an appalachian holy roller mob

how i miss that old ritual
with irReverend grace slick scowling
all i did for easter was paint some eggs!
stupid christian! no more nails,
no more nails in his holy legs!

nothingwoman

i am nothingwoman
gouged out, emptied, down
as low/as i/can go
(it happens this wa
once in awhile)
high hopes imploded
SOLID turned to b l o w n   d u s t
can't find one speck
to hold onto--
let me tell you
i'd do anything, ANYthing
to be anywhere but here
yet I won't leave
'cause only when I'm nothingwoman
only in this empty place
am I still enough to hear the whisper:

god will dream you new again

transforming scars to art

in fairy tales it's easy to spin straw to gold
but here on the ground where slaves and survivors
must grind through what we grind through
there's not the least fiction when we transform scars to art
when we write it and paint it and sing it to beauty despite.

despite everything that had to be heaved through
despite the desperate prayers
despite our weary shoulders
there came that point of lightning that renewed us
that inspiration on how to make it
something else entirely
and we just knew.

and everything flowed from pen and brush and
from voices rooted in the pain of birth
crying out for life, for life, for life sublime

oh no, there's not the least fiction when we
transform scars to art
they're by far the truest stories ever told

i will smoke again before i die

i will smoke again before i die

but it will not be tobacco in my pipe
no, it will be old hurts consumed, ascending
wisping out into the ethers
it will be all those judgments
of who and what was good for me in life
who and what was bad
it will be all those times i
clung to people places and things
all those times i wearied
and wanted to let go—but couldn't
it will be every useless worry
that never came to pass
it will be every quiet sadness
every disappointment
every insult
every shock
every hard cry

it will be all those false politenesses

all those heavy pressures to repress truths
will reduce to ash and blow away
gone all posturing and strutting just
to cover up the toxic shame infection
i will burn that shame to cinder too
my pipe will be fueled by all those barriers
that kept me so long from
loving this and that about myself
i will burn off all blaming, all projections
i will burn off all the anger and armor that came
from dreaming myself small or in danger
i will burn away excesses:
misinformation medication
illusions expectations
i will leave this life
lean and burned pure to the core
taking with me only what i brought
leaving behind a simple one syllable kiss
that the face of the world will know only as

love

out of shadows,
up from graves

warning: beyond this fence is a military installation

i walk my dogs in the shadow
of the apocalypse
steps from the guarded caves
where two thousand nightmares
dream their fitful dreams
of turning skies into mass graves
for babies   vaporized mid-coo
for young mothers
with so much love in their eyes
for exuberant puppies
bounding through the beginnings of life
for the dreams of cities
island nations
whole civilizations

across the fence from where i stand
prairie dogs scan the sands
for signs of approaching coyotes
glance skyward for winged predators
that may swoop down on them in a flash
doing their best to protect themselves
and their little ones
living their lives
   burrowed
        like me
in the shadow of the apocalypse

Will and Pablo
for Will Inman

Will, when you still lived in that trailer on
mossman road you sent me a box of your
poems all brimming with kauris and
truth turtles and roots twitching with
god-in-man, will-in-man blooming
irises crashing waves against
Lady Liberty claiming the fifth (not
beethoven's) and tongues surfed and
Isaac and Abraham new covenants
in the deep south, dark mother gods
yearning out of their suffering to pray

Is there ever too much love in the world?

man-man love and you singing singing to
crescendos of I AM HUMAN FIRST piercing
the crusted frail skins of the twentieth
century to reach your accidental son and
birth yourself from suicide blood

all this in scattered bits of paper and
journals and egghunts through so many
poems to find your oval fertilities
in this *lucid stone* and that *umbra*

i have coaxed your rainbow from the box but
i have just one question   why
did you include styrofoam in a box of paper
do you still feel your beauty
fragile/is there some fear that
lingers—of FBI and house subcommittees
that may come to crush, interrogate?
nothing can destroy your vision now
that it is loosed on gull wings to
fly above the molten ocean solid

solid like Neruda's ghost

women when we rise

women, when we rise we rise heaving
panting, pushing, screaming like
big bang birthing, when we rise
women, when we rise we rise against
pain, through pain, through pain,
through more pain than one body
can stand it seems

women, when we rise it's never just
one resurrection it's always
bringing more life with it,
pulling the whole underworld along
it's bursting tombs into
seedlings and springtime and
singing tomorrows when we rise

women, when we rise truth mountains
shadow-darkened for centuries
burst watermelon and high-lit ribs
plain as day for a hundred miles
when we rise
women, when we rise
secrets cry out from crevices
sulphured springs transform to sparkling,
what once was poison now is fuel
for still more rising when we rise

women, when we rise there is no
wind can take us down
tethered as we are to moon and myst'ry
women, when we rise all else is trifled:
all the foulest deeds of greed and war
all fears that spawn them gone
when women find their power

women, when we rise we rise together
out of bones unnamed and cries forgotten
bonded to our cells like
witch to stake, like slave to chain,
like hiroshima vapor to the stone,
like juarez blood to desert sand
but when we rise we bring them every soul
from the first mother forward

and goddess breath will roar from us forever
when we rise

women, when we rise we must not,
cannot, will not be put down again
when women rise
when women—
women rise!

terri who?

i can't care too much
about the terri schiavo spectacle
i care, but i can't care too much
about her parents' pain
not when a poor woman in my own downtown today
rose slowly from low on the curb
her untelevised sorrows weighing her hips
too dense to vent in tears
        deep and unnoticed
                not even named…
she's lost a son to street violence
the dangerous game of poverty
it happened six gray years ago today
she's the only one who thinks of his sweet face
remembrin how he'd cool her fevered brow
and now she must get up and catch the bus alone

another string of dull black pearls
that even when together   they're apart
                those are her days…
and ain't no president sayin nuthin
about her pain

this Heart

i know you hold all the warheads
all the locks on prison cells
all the fingers on all the triggers
but this Heart knows what it knows

this Heart beats the rhythm joy
the tender mother melody
the easy harmony of children at play
this Heart rides bass notes through black canyons
dances the piccolos of stars
blooms delicacy and beauty in places
no human eye has witnessed
this Heart plunges oceans purple deep with loss
only to splash across the sky in brilliant rose
horizon to horizon

this Heart knows what it knows
what can you do with this Heart?
think you can regulate, violate, subjugate,
obliterate this Heart?
just *try* to crush it in your brutish hands
and it will spill to spawn ten thousand more

oh I know you hoard all the measurable treasure
and belittle those you stole it from
but you cannot begin to secure this Heart
not this Heart, not by violence nor propaganda
this Heart knows what it knows
this Heart is not for sale at any price
nobody's property, least of all yours

this Heart will go on and on to the beat of
unrelenting truth, quickening to love
stopping for no one, this Heart
i know you're planning how you will
eventually own it all or destroy it all
you have it all figured out, don't you?

but you have no experts, no agencies, no authorities
who can remotely calculate this Heart
you can pool your best military strategists
unleash your most massive weapons
but they cannot touch, much less destroy, this Heart

when you pound your puny chest
beat your drums of war
march out your million murdering slaves
across the soil and sea
know that this Heart does not flinch

and as your empire sinks for the third time
in the arrogance of its own imperialism
the very last sound in your dying ears
will be the beat, the beat, the sweet immortal beat of
this Heart

savior shigeko-san

today i met a savior, shigeko sasamori
only 13 her first day sweeping the streets of hiroshima
august sixth 1945

little boy dropped, she went down twice
but came back up again

then down under the surgeon's knife
to reconstruct, to reconstruct until
here she {almost} is again

sight of that plane in the smithsonian
it makes her brain go white to see
sixty years later

but here she is in new mexico
birthplace of the bomb
and laughs, and clutches her horror to her forehead

shigeko tells her story

i'm not just here saying i'm a victim of hiroshima—look at me
no, i know a lot of americans died
a lot of koreans, brazileans, and all kinds of people die from war

i'm saying look at the babies
nobody says, oh a baby, get that away from me
no, we smile and say aw! a baby!
and that baby's doing its job already
i'm saying we have to end war, all war
for them—for the babies
i ask people, do you have any grandchildren
what kind of a world do you want to leave to them?

and when I go in the schools i tell the young people
don't go in the military, it's very simple
how could they have a war if there weren't any soldiers?
and they say no, no we won't

she laughs, this tiny savior
oh, the young people, they are so cute

shigeko the lowly, come to absolve us of our sins
and from those awful scars shines ample love to save us
do we deserve so much forgiveness
and will we go and sin no more?

bomb blast goggles

even with these goggles and my eyes closed
i can see the bones in my own arm
the science is amazing
the science is amazing!
the sun rose twice today
thanks to the Trinity
Truman Groves Oppenheimer
Allelujah! Allelujah!
the science is amazing!
E=mc squared minus 140 thousand innocents—Hiroshima
E=mc squared minus 70 thousand more innocents—Nagasaki
E=mc squared minus 1 John Wayne—Nevada
E=mc squared minus who knows how many navajo uranium
miners—buried on the rez
E=mc squared plus Chernobyl, plus Three Mile Island,
plus depleted uranium
plus nuclear waste—toxic for 144 thousand years

plus leukemia, plus thyroid cancer, plus prostate cancer, plus
breast cancer
plus babies born without brains
plus babies born with major organs outside their bodies
plus, plus…
but why go on? why add it all up?
the science is amazing
all i can see is
the science is amazing

on numbers

i like the sound of one hundred thirty two
in vietnamese: mot tram ba moi hai
the rhythm of it, two dotted whole notes
followed by three eighth notes
strong then fast, the song of southest asia
mostly i don't like numbers themselves
just their names—and not in english
the way they rhyme in spanish, one to six
uno dos tres/quatro cinco seis
like some mariachi step
or the staccato japanese one to five
ichi ni san shi go
three fast, three slow
like chin-style tai chi
and the german ones so blunt and guttural
ein zwei drei fier fumpf
i can almost see the dough-faced children
playing by the rhine, jumping rope or
whatever german children do these days
but in my checkbook ledger,
my paystubs, my bank statements,
the bills that pass through my mailbox,
in and out again, numbers count my days,
my life energy exchanged for stark syllables:
one and two and three and four and five and six

somebody said he liked numbers best
'cause numbers never lie but
to me they are the biggest lies of all
assigned to my account by hour or week or month or service
rendered
then traded back for food, shelter, comfort, toys
(enough assigned and some claim brutal power)

tell me, what do numbers truly have to do with worth?

yes, i like the sound of one hundred thirty two
in vietnamese: not the quantity it represents but
the rhythm of slight bronze-skinned hands in water:
mot tram ba moi hai
mot tram ba moi hai
mot tram ba moi hai

McJesus

i reached Jesus on His cellphone
i needed ten minutes of facetime
but He was between appointments
you know how it is—God has His busy days
i said i understood and broke down crying
so He said, aw, call me   maybe I can meet with you on Thursday
I left my palm pilot in my other coat
or email me tonight, let's talk about it
but I just can't meet with you today

i was disappointed but i understood
His McCaring schedule's full
i thought maybe He'd call me to check in later but
i guess He forgot about me
or just figured i'd be fine

so i called today but got His voicemail
and i didn't leave a message
—don't wanna bother God—i know
it's hard to do compassion in this modern world
—so many needs!
a person's gotta know their limits and
take care of themselves, even Jesus—especially Jesus!

sometimes it's just easier to write a check for
what you care about, you know?
—can't do it all!
so i have faith that when Jesus gets a moment
He'll make a generous donation
to crisis intervention if He can

i am a poet

i am a poet to reclaim the ravages of war
to amplify the human heartbeat in the chest of the enemy
to remind the soldier that he once was a child who dissolved into sobs
at the death of a dog

i am a poet to reclaim the ravages of war
rained by one race, one religion on another
sometimes between nations
sometimes within them
i cut all skins and mingle the red blood indistinguishable on the page
i fuse all prayers into one chant of longing for a justice, a goodness
that yet eludes us

i am a poet to reclaim the ravages of war
to pluck the child from beneath the bruising arm of rage
to pluck the woman from the path of rape's intruding missile
to hold them up in sundrenched mist where they can sparkle golden
and untarnished as the day they burst this world a breath of god

i am a poet to reclaim humanity from the ravages of war
not to count the casualties but to heal them

i am a poet and my task is immense
i cannot do it alone
but an army of poets can kiss the world awake

gaza lament

if the palestinians and the israelis
had been reading each other poetry all these years
they'd be in love by now

i can't hear of all this war
all this unneccessary
of people so sick from fear
old fears still diseasing
new fears louder than thunder
(nothing scarier than scar tissue
ripped into new flesh)

child eyes, living and dead, fixed on us
demand a different answer

i can't bear the thought of children
terrified by terrified men
bombing down their terrible fear on cities
cities filled with their sisters
filled with their brothers
cities filled with themselves
if they only could see

maybe someday their grandchildren
won't speak to them for shame
maybe someday they'll be as lonely
as old germans are now

harry who cares

it's a biography narrated over swing
        bop-bah doppa dop DOP
        bop-bah doppa dop DOP
what an unlikely candidate
to take over for the great roosevelt

what an unlikely candidate
to use the most terrible weapon devised by man
        bop-bah doppa dop DOP
        bop-bah doppa dop DOP
and i hear the words of the shaveheaded
African daughter:
        limelight's been on the white men
        far too long
and the documentary declares
        he was bankrupt at thirty-six
        all bankrupt   completely bankrupt
        bop-bah doppa dop DOP
        bop-bah doppa dop DOP
and the young medical student declares
from beneath her blonde wings:
        they're completely against
        all natural laws
and bob kerry walks around
in the madness of no guilt all these years
and the skull and bones
neophytes chant:
        the hangman equals death
        the devil equals death
        death equals death

if i weren't menopausal
i'd squeeze out a messiah who
would resurrect all the flesh of
        hiroshima and nagasaki and auschwitz and sand creek and
        the middle passage and the trail of tears and mylai and the
        Chilean
        disappeared and rigoberta's family and the children of
        jenin and the young gods of AIDS
                                yes She would!
they'd rise from my old womb to
my throat and i'd cry out in blissful travail
and we'd dance together a billion strong

for centuries of mornings in the Garden
          bop-bah doppa dop DOP
          bop-bah doppa dop DOP
          bop-bah doppa dop DOP
          bop-bah doppa dop DOP
          bop-bah doppa dop DOP
     now *there's* a scene Worthy of the soundtrack

suspect

am i mexican? no
am i a citizen? yes
so why are *my* eyes welling up, arizona?
why is *my* stomach churned?
my soul disturbed?

you sent me back, arizona, on that cross-country trip
back to that stop in topeka
on a greyhound where i swear some white frat boys
from UNLV gave a girl a date rape drug the night before
one big guy's legs across the aisle
kept anyone from going back there
nothing was done.

but in the daylight in topeka
me in my blue chinese hat, a gift
some friends found at a flea market
covered in brightly-colored pins:
red stars, chinese flags, flowers, idyllic asian scenes
to me it was whimsical
to the two pistoled cops, sheriff K-9 unit on their buckles
white shirts, blue pants tucked inside their army boots
one with a shaved head—
that hat was nothing you could buy at k-mart
to them it shouted commie! chinese! illegal! suspect!
threat! up to no good!
so one demanded WHERE YOU FROM, HUH?
while the other rifled through my bags stuffed overhead
oh yeah, maybe the frat boys would have asked for
a search warrant but i answered politely as i could
heart pounding/cheeks flushed/gun inches from my head
WHERE DID YOU BOARD THIS BUS?
WHY WERE YOU IN COLORADO?
WHERE YOU GETTING OFF?
all the while snooping through my bags
like my clothes were contraband

finally satisfied that i spoke fluent english
carried no sayings of chairman mao
no materials to make a bomb
they moved on to their only other target:
YOU SPEAK ENGLISH? they demanded
YOU GOT A GREEN CARD?

WHERE'S YOUR GREEN CARD?
LET ME SEE YOUR GREEN CARD NOW!
yes yes yes
scrambling to retrieve it from his pocket trembling

white passengers kept reading or looking out the window
as if they didn't see or hear a thing
a few old african americans sat there tired, resigned,
expecting to be next/relieved they weren't this time

i watched from the window as he got off the bus next stop
heard him speaking spanish to the woman waiting
she all ears and upset eyes

someone said we know how fascist the government is
by how much we fear the police

funny how topeka is suddenly berlin
the star of david, pink triangle there
here it's your green card, your english and your papers
and they better be just right

we're all jews sometimes, all gay and
arizona, you have made us all illegals
with your flimsy mere suspicions
with your hatred for the "other"
buckled in and booted down
am i mexican? yes
am i a citizen? no
not in arizona
not in arizona, no!
not in a state so far from grace

final station of the cross

She hangs suspended in space
Her head bowed with a crown of
carbon dioxide and CFCs
Her side speared by stripmines
abandoned drilling sites
nuclear waste depositories
Her faithful Whale children
beach themselves in desperate protest
but to no avail
Her faithful mountain keepers
come down from the Andes to
warn their wayward brothers
Her northern children cry out
from their irradiated Reindeer,
their disappearing Glaciers

and She cries out for Her lost children too
        oh Florida Red Wolf! oh Arizona Jaguar!
        oh Monk Seal! oh Heath Hen! She cries

        where is my Mysterious Starling? my Great Elephantbird?
        my Red Colobus Monkey? my Laughing Owl?
        Clear Lake Splittail?   Caspian Tiger?
        Mexican Grizzly Bear?   Spanish Wolf?   Dwarf
        Hippopotamus? Sumatran Lion? Eastern Elk?
        LabradorDuck?JapaneseSeaLion?NewZealandQuail???

        why can't I find my Sea Mink? my Barbary Lion?
        my Ivory-Billed Woodpecker? my Hopping Mouse?

        why have my children forsaken me?

but only silence—
{silence}
echoes from extinction's unmarked graves

and She dies more and more and more alone each hour
with none left to forgive the offending human child
judas to us all/ the mad marauder who
cannot wash his guilty hands in toxic waste
whose silver cities will be cast aside like sins whose
missile silos will no longer gleam in that dark hour who
too will die when She cries
              IT IS FINISHED!
for he, the fool, is in his Mother's womb

down on diamonds
(stormsong)

he thinks he forced us down
down on our knees to scrub his floors
down on the bed to bear his soldiers
down in the underclass, the underground, the underbelly
down in his prison cells
down on his payroll
down in the realm of animal, of slave, of account number, of soul-less
down to the subservience of his name, his dollar bill, his god

he thinks he forced us down
down and out on the streets
down in the crackhouses, the homeless shelters
down to beg him for a handout
down on the sofa by the tv
down where we can't see through smoke and mirrors
down where we can't hear anyone cry
for the blare of the commercials
down where we believe we're not good enough, not thin enough,
        not rich enough,
not pretty enough, not blonde enough, not white enough
                                            not enough

he thinks he forced us down
    down on our knees to service him, stiff and sadistic, while
feigning compassion

he thinks he forced us down
into invisibility, to silence, complicity, help-less-ness
and maybe we have buckled a time or two
maybe we've bowed here and there to survive but

our knees are boned in diamonds
our spines are solid gold
we'll never tarnish, never cheapen
never stay bent for a moment longer than necessary
he has no eyes to see us strolling the galaxies
birthing stars and moons and sapphires
our skin rich with the silk of centuries
our blood, ancient as amber
our hands, strong as jade and ivory
he has no ears to hear
the song of our souls

voices of generations past and
multitudes yet to be born
in chorus that cannot be charted
on his meager scale from *do* to *do*

perhaps he hears the refrain like
          thunder on the edge of his treachery
perhaps he now fortifies his armory
strikes violent blows in
one last desperate flail to
push it down to hold it back to keep control
of what was never his, of what
has always soared above him, escaped
          behind him   slipped away
try as he may

Mother, for the sake of all those times we
          knelt and wept on diamonds
for all those times we worked away the silk
          to barest jade
Mother! Mother! this time do not spare him
we'll gladly stand and face the lightning
while the cleansing storm rolls in

don't ask don't tell

don't ask don't tell me
of your drone missile strikes
launched from an air-conditioned office
somewhere in the american west
as if our soldiers are playing video games
then going home to have dinner with their families
like it was nothing at all

don't ask don't tell me
of your pro-life stance
when you cheer the shock and awe
that kills thousands of fetuses
along with their expectant mothers
toddling sisters
curly-haired brothers
all in a quest for barrels of oil
don't ask don't even tell me, please

don't ask don't tell
of your good wars
when i come from
a japanese girl traumatized
by the burning rain of napalm
and a farmboy haunted a lifetime
by his buddy throwing scalding water
in the faces of children
foraging through garbage for food
yes, my dad told me
he got down on his knees and begged god
to return some compassion to his heart
before he returned stateside
after all he'd seen
don't ask don't tell me
of your so-called good wars

don't ask don't tell
of the billions and billions and billions
siphoned from busboys and schoolteachers
nurses and construction workers
firefighters and waitresses
administrative assistants and truck drivers
plumbers and retail clerks
to fund military bases all over the world and

corporate towers to protect the untouchable royalty
of military contractors and
fat dividends for the lazy rich who
invest their ancestors' spoils of
slavery and native blood
while twenty-four thousand children starve every day
prisons are bulging in their millions
healthcare and education are chronically underfunded

don't ask don't tell me
of a father and son
filthy in oil and fascism
who appoint supreme court justices
who rule that money is speech
to ensure that the people
never again get in their measly two cents

and for sure don't ask don't tell me
how a man who loves another man
a woman who loves another woman
aren't fit to serve
i wish with all my heart
they didn't even want to

don't ask don't tell me
how sacred it is
to feed ourselves to a greedy monster
that never once thinks to ask
that never wants us to tell
what's really truly going on in america

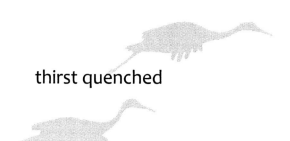

thirst quenched

ask alice

i remember reading
through the looking glass
with a friend
my first female lover
we both liked vonnegut
and lewis carroll
our favorite saying
was the red queen quotation
when she gave alice a dry biscuit:

thirst quenched i hope?

tail end hippies
in the late seventies
trying out a new kinda love
she taught me how to kiss
and i knew from the very first one:

no dry biscuits here

magic trilogy

magic 1.
gay people, we're magical
we've been seduced by life
by art   by the beauty of earth
and each other
we listen for the subtle
tones of romance
we capture it in words
and looks and dances
in the way we touch
the way we speak of touch
we refuse the coffin of normalcy
we refuse to look and not see
life itself is beautifully abnormal
don't you think?
each generation gets it again
it feels so good
when those passing it to the future
respect the ones who've gone before
the old ones respect and praise
amazed at the young ones' gifts
how grand life rolls on
crashing in on itself
back out again

magic 2.
women intrigue me   so complex
myself included
i know the power of being a woman
yet understand how a man must feel
sometimes the "he" possesses me
my voice lowers
there's nothing i wouldn't do
to be inside a woman
i completely understand that
other times the power of surrender
is what i crave

magic 3.
i dressed like a man
this halloween
though i had planned to go
as a geisha

i'm fifty and i could be seductive
either way
it's all about the power of art
i live to give it
a thousand voices
on every street
no need to fear me
i am more seduced by it
than i can use it to seduce
it's for us all i want to
reach every ear i can
with the seductive power of art
made strong by all our
ways of being human
because i believe that art—
if it can find enough tongues
to speak it true—
is that magic that still could save us all
at this late hour

she parted the afternoon

she parted the afternoon
to lay a dozen long-stemmed
miracles at my feet
crimson, they were, like the
passion of her soft petal lips
kissed by baby's breath
a woman's moist longing
clinging to their stems
the fragrance curling
around my ankles
my calves, my thighs
her approaching lips
parting mine
    and so surrounded
i completely surrendered
had i been the powerful
Nefertiti i would have
gladly followed her
into the folding sea

we met around the sacred fire

we met around the sacred fire of poetry
and you haven't missed one since
                                    until tonight
it didn't matter that they clapped
didn't matter that the old men showed respect
didn't matter that the women smiled broadly
proudly introduced me to their sons and friends
a hole the size of you kept calling from the darkness
and found that empty echo in the hollow of my heart
i drove home alone   missing you
knowing you are far out of my orbit now for sure
no gravitational pull
no irresistible force field
it's all distant and igloo
you frame it like you're protecting us both
like together we're the death star
but i was once the golden sun with you, the
poet laureate of your heart
that's what you called me many times:
Poet Laureate of My Heart

i loved that name.

i consider wearing a t-shirt that says if you're attracted to me you must need a shrink

case 1. what i want

don't get me wrong
i'm not picky
just don't send me cultists
or alcoholics
or those with anger issues
undiagnosed bipolars
perhaps worse: those who have
pilled away their drive

send me somebody truly kind
with beauty that shines from her
from an artist's soul and a wizard's mind
i'm not that picky
i just want romance. respect
as deep as lust is high

case 2. my ex from the bronx

she said you're gonna keep attracting these bugouts
until you learn the lesson they have for you
and that is: when you gonna take power
over your own life?
how long you gonna let these bugout women
have power over you?

(geez, i wish she would have given me this lecture
when she was the "bugout" with power over me)

she's right that i keep dancing that
same old backwards dance
deferring to people far less equipped to lead

for what? are you afraid they'll leave you
all alone? she demands
come out of fear! her parting words
as she walks weaponed into night

case 3. then there's this woman
who acts like she wants me but

isn't done wanting her ex
doesn't want me
now she wants me
now she moves her ex back in
where am i? she wants me.
she wants me? what? who?
who does she want? where am I again?

case 4. fragile: handle with care until *you're* broken

what i learned from this one:
body/mind/spirit are indeed all one
(except in cases where they're not)
nothing says nice girls can't be narcissistic
(although it does seem to keep them
from recognizing that they are)
but the most disquieting lesson is:
i far too easily fall down that rabbit hole again

case 5. well apparently i'm it.

universal spelunk

what commands me—
the seizure of longings within my chest or
the steady scraping of whispers against my skull.
if only the Deity would
    announce herself in singular contralto,
not lose herself in a chorus of
    mores, instincts, marketing ploys,
        social agendas.
    i am weary of sorting and
        weeding and straining and
where is the cave where silence speaks
a solo in clearest azure tone
that carries to the hem of the
                                farthest star
this speck yearns to synthesize,
        simplify
hum the Goddess note eternal